The Earth Will Outshine Us

Also by Kathryn Fry and published by Ginninderra Press
Green Point Bearings

Kathryn Fry

The Earth Will Outshine Us

For my family
especially Ian

The Earth Will Outshine Us
ISBN 978 1 76109 171 1
Copyright © Kathryn Fry 2021
Cover image taken by the author from the Krichauff Range,
Northern Territory

First published 2021 by
GINNINDERRA PRESS
PO Box 3461 Port Adelaide 5015
www.ginninderrapress.com.au

Contents

The Way In
    KI Postscript   9
    Going Home   10
    Circuit, Blackheath   11
    The Way In   12
    Underground   13
    Down from Dorrigo   14
    With the Moths on Ash Island   15
    The Matter of Covid-19   16

The Art of Doing Things
    Under the Microscope   19
    April, Merewether   24
    The Balance   25
    Fluid Icons   26
    About the Centre, Even Now   28
    Ocean Face, Ocean Mind   30
    The Art of Doing Things   31
    Resolution   32
    Olive with Still Life   33
    The Means to the End   34
    Artistry   36

The Earth Will Outshine Us
    The Lesson   39
    The Earth Will Outshine Us   40
    Beneath the Blue Quandong   41
    Links   42
    On William Robinson's Later Harvest   43
    In Silence   44
    Hearing the Grey   45

   From On High   46
   In Tumult   48
   Green Tea   49

Skin to Skin

   Blaze and Stone   53
   Swifts in the Sclerophyll   54
   Facing the Music   55
   In Our Name   56
   Beef Tea Heirloom   57
   St Lucia, 1969   58
   Her Hands   59
   Greengrocer   60
   Skin to Skin   61
   Toddler with Neptune's Necklace   62
   Now She's Three   63
   Now She's Four   65

Track Drift

   Waiting   69
   Walking   70
   Reunion   71
   Trees   72
   Beech (*Fagus sylvatica*)   74
   By the Hawkesbury   75
   Track Drift   76
   Foresight   77
   Chaos on a Canvas   78
   Notes   80
   Acknowledgements   81

The Way In

KI Postscript

The day we stood under the canopies of sugar gums
cooling the Playford Highway and caught the look of

a sand goanna: his dusky skin banded in code to the tail,
the dots of white on his legs, the sharp line of his lips.

Beyond some spheres of tufted grass trees, there half-
way up a brown stringybark, a huddle of thick-coated fur.

We drove to the heath at the edge of the land, dense
with slender honey myrtle, coast boobialla and more

we couldn't name; and a wallaby paused by a sweep
of low mounds and bird calls. That day we stepped

easy among the matrix of living things, seeing some
of the island's web – all the day's colours as spirited

as the lustre of the deep aqua Southern Ocean. But
now our mainland screens show ash and black loss,

the soil that held life there, surely sterile. Our mouths
are struck mute, our minds full of the clamour of fire.

Going Home

In memory of J.O'Flaherty

She breathes the air of her forebears
and walks the muddied path to the ruins

of the Cleared Coast, the hills lit by ling
heather. She hears of crofters once turfed out,

of their evictors wasting basins of milk,
yes, milk to douse the fire in the hearths

of homes in Boreraig. And of the wailing
and wandering by the waters of Loch Eishort.

But now in the southern spring sky of her
homeland, walls of flame lap at the edge

of old rainforest – the heritage house ablaze
and tumbling – and all the burning sears her

here as streams channel down by granite, and
gleam by bog myrtle, blaeberry and Scots pine.

Circuit, Blackheath

Just yesterday there was no hint of these
tenuous doubletail orchids on stray stems

and overnight, the waratah's central bloom
morphed into steady shoots, triggered

by the promise of rain, it seems. I think
how different we are, you and I, often

on separate paths. This morning, a hillside's
lit with a thousand lanterns of bauera rose,

another with yellow peas in the grey light,
the air awash with peppermint oil. Whistlers

and spinebills sing up and down the track
and the creek runs louder at Boyds Beach.

We meet on this day in November, attuned to
each other at Govetts Leap, before the megafire

burns from Gospers Mountain and blazes Grose
Valley and sweeps up the cliffs at Blackheath.

The Way In

After Danie Mellor's *Landstory* (2018)

You've never sat against a ribbonwood
    braiding fibre into a dilly bag,
never leached cycad seeds in the reaches
    of a creek, never stepped barefoot
upriver for the succulent hearts of palms.
    You've no age-old link to the land,
with its hold like an owning; your elders were
    urban dwellers. Yet here you are,
before the gnarled bark of a satinash, its red
    fruit ripe by your feet, as you search
for a way into the depths of this forest, a track
    beyond the fallen trunk, the chatter
of a chowchilla nearby. You want to be grounded
    in bush and its stories. You've come
in a time of heady world angst, its souring turmoil.
    Here there's no road, no building, no
dahlia, no jacaranda. There's nothing arid in
    the sweep of green as you gaze about.
You want to be out of the rush for somewhere
    else, your mind empty of any
catastrophe it cares to conjure. You want to be
    open to the opulence,
to breathe among the figs and king ferns.

Underground

They break the air so high – like the slow sound
of a pied butcher-bird, like the young on a quest
for the world to join before the heat swells –
the Gymea lily up Awaba way, a forest full like
all the moments in your life. They look tame

yet one by one come autumn after the smoke's
settled, they thrust a spear of a stem or more
and the crown thickens to a fistful filling by spring,
the head a bowl of scarlet swollen with pollen
dangling in green about the openings. These

flame lilies will persist you think (deep-rooted,
drought-hardy); you search for a likeness given
the carbon turmoil – your hands perhaps, lilied
with years of touch or some inner place like
the lily's bulb underground, something to tap into.

Down from Dorrigo

Had you not come here you'd have missed
the red drift down from an Illawarra flame,
the cream of a yellow carabeen on the forest

floor and the untold shades and shapes like
thoughts in the continual clamour for power.
Insects swirl where the sun filters through

and you remember those who lightened your
path. Birds ripple and render the air and you
wonder will they always. Had you not come

here you'd have missed the fluency of palms
and vines and those old, overpowering trunks.
Now your mind hovers on a draught of hope.

With the Moths on Ash Island

Harriet Scott has spent the day with the Emperor, her brush whispering precise colours to the page, every stage of its silenced life down to each larval hair. The zigzag markings of outstretched wings, the plump flesh, the feathered antennae. She sets her brush on the bench and strides out into the whirr of wings about the mangroves by the Hunter River. As if the air hums in its own wind, an eddy here and there as moths fan close to her ear though none bruise her face. In the distance, water birds settle, the heat muffling their cries. So many quiet hours with the moths on Ash Island for this, her notable work. Her thoughts ring with impatience; she says it out loud and later writes it in her letter to Edward Ramsay, *Clearly I ought to have been Harry Scott instead of Hattie.*

The Matter of Covid-19

I follow butterflies up a rise to snap
    a shot of them. As I walk, two or three
suddenly lift out of their folded selves,
    their black, twig-like striations
of camouflage undone. Then their flights,
    waving the air as if conducting music
and the flicker of white spans as they
    search for one another, a game of chase
and choice and chance as it's always
    been. So many of them about the reserve
this mild autumn day, the same day our
    country closed borders because of a much
smaller thing, not living of itself (no breath,
    no song) and so small, billions could crown
a tiny pierid's wing, and so alarming,
    its microscopic strands of novel bio-code
would set a blind course of human skittles.

The Art of Doing Things

Under the Microscope

'In the 1920s, it was the only thing a woman without an education could do. That and Nursing.' – Isobel Bennett AO (1909–2008)

Part 1 The Christmas Cruise

William J. Dakin meets Isobel and her sister
at boat drill, his wife by his side, his voice
ruffling the deck of the P&O *Straithaird*.

They kept a friendly eye on us, she writes.
Isobel, twenty-three and out of work,
learns of the world in the word 'zoology'.

Part 2 *It was all a matter of practice*

i

Professor Dakin invites his secretary, Isobel,
to focus on the microscope. And she joins
the crew of the *Thistle* vessel, sea legs steady

even up the mast with brush and varnish.
She hauls in the silk net from Broken Bay
to sort, to study, to sum the catch

on the laboratory bench. Month by month
records grow, the script becomes a monograph
becomes the reference, a standard like gold.

ii

They sift king prawns in Lake Illawarra.
Phenomenal win they offer fishery: find
prawns large as young lobsters, out at sea.

iii

Isobel considers the craft of concealment:
a crab fixing grit or sponge bits to its carapace,
the stick insect, chromatophores of cuttlefish,

a sand-coloured goby in the sand, the leafy sea
dragon, how squid by the bombora turn to water
and back again, their eyes set on her stance.

> *Meticulous in everything he did, mercurial*
> *in temperament. Forthright. Irrepressible.*
> *Enough was never enough for Professor Dakin.*

After the war, Isobel and three zoologists pack
the 1940 Ford sloper: boot stacked with ropes,
nets and lidded jars; tents and cases on the roof

rack, hats and oranges on the back shelf. Going
north to Coolangatta for a dozen coastal points;
ninety species she'll register at Merewether.

iv

You haven't lived
until you've seen a sea-worm
under the microscope.

At Gorgonia Hole, in clear twenty-four
degrees with little current, she floats
in the thrill of flying without the fall.

Only the light drops in long shafts
down the blue. There among the sculptures
of limestone, as if she's before the birth

of fish stripe and dash and swirl in
black, scarlet, orange; that pea-green
parrotfish aslant in a trance by streaks

of cleaner wrasse (how he shimmies
when they're done), the school in flicks
of pink, lemon and mother-of-pearl.

In the shallows, two turtles are mating;
the female gasps air and groans into
the long and moonlit hours.

V

> *I have rockhopped from Double Island Point*
> *to southern Tasmania, from Wilsons Prom*
> *to the Leeuwin and north in WA...*

See her combing mainland shores and islands:
Heron, Lord Howe, the Low Isles, Macquarie,
Maatsuyker, Kangaroo; the list is long.

Picture her with upturned boulders by reef or
tidal pool, to count worms, tunicates, and sponge;
showing students the shapes and singularities

in the zones and among the fronds. Faux play
in shallow brine near that wild swirl about
the coral or cunjevoi or kelp. Hear her: how

a sea star cut in half becomes two; the crabs'
moult and couple, the moonlight trigger of
a coral cloud, squid's quick clasp and dump,

a sea hare's eggs on a string, the sea squirts'
release and the common toados'. See her over
the oceans in a floating class on the *Te Vega*,

and the *Galathea*, or the descent to Kieta
as the plane circles over sand cays and reefs;
how she notes in Arawa Bay: dolphins and

tuna preying on small fish gorging
on a swarm of larvae, terns diving into the mix
and taken in turn by frigates on the wing.

Part 3 Legacy

Who can't love the wafting nudibranchs,
the shell-less slugs, like *Glaucus*, little drifters
of decoy: lapis-back, a blind for the birds,

silver-under to fool the fish; smaller than
a child's thumb, its stomach slips the stinging
cells of a bluebottle into its own defence.

Pretty on the cover for Isobel's ninetieth.
And there's her photo, a gilded *Glaucus*
pinned to her red cardigan, her papers soon

for the nation's archive, the boxes loaded
for the trolley. Nine books, one reef,
one genus, five species, carry her name.

> *One expects to quietly fade away and be*
> *forgotten, but with the Mueller Medal*
> *I felt I had joined the immortals.*

April, Merewether

An octopus slides along a channel of water,
its blue rings unfazed in the mild autumn sun
of a midday at Merewether. A crab settles

the bulk of its red body into a crevice
and a myriad of single-valved wanderers
abound around the pools, among the baubles

and bladders, the green sea fingers and straps,
the coralline pinks and a few tropical fronds
in the cradlings. Two boys prod at sea hares;

a girl gathers cushion stars. No longer
the number of species listed in '46; cart-rut
shells lie empty, turban snails have gone.

The Balance

His bag swells with a clutch of turban snails,
each moonfaced lid sucked against its flesh.

So skilled, he collects on the ebb of a spring tide,
the rock shelf exposed, the water calm.

His eyes scoff at the coastguards' *leave
some for your children, your future and ours.*

Later they find only one such mollusc –
whorled to a tip, its heart fine-tuned to roam

and crop the algae. That day and the next, others
comb the platform, tilting the balance.

Fluid Icons

After Judy Watson's *heron island suite* (2009)

There's a lens of freshwater, a chalice
of trapped rain, increasing in density
down to the sea and ready for the gain

to the roots of the Pisonia forest, and
the many black noddies, seated nun-like,
white-wimpled, on duty in October nests.

But it's February now, the chicks hatched, or
with wings sticky with seed, they're sacrificed
fodder for the cycles to follow. This should

never end you think, the green turtles blessing
us with hatchlings, and the birds, flying out,
flying in to join the presiding flock of silvereyes.

In the water, you're a celebrant at the altar
of coral plates, domes and fans, of branches,
ridges and fleshy fingers; and the rippling

colours about the lips of clams and bevy
of fish in their tugging frenzy. Such purpose
and pace and susurrus of the place.

And you think of the sacred waters of Lawn Hill,
the land recovering from the direst fire, over
a million hectares burnt. You watched archer fish

cruise around lilies, reverent in the snake-like creek;
you walked in rising heat above the green-jewelled
gorge, each bird's call a new hymn. But in the dry

lab of this island, you view graphs and charts,
the intervals and lines of best fit to dream by.
The holy grail of data from studies over the years

should be enough, you hope, to keep loss at bay,
to keep the seas from rising, our hearts from writhing.
Today with fragments from the sand, you're a witness

to the history in a shark's purse, in a nub of coral,
in the wind-torn leaves of native bay cedar and
a gull's feather you gather in the day's closing shades.

About the Centre, Even Now

i Desert Oak

The way you bend to sweep your hand
through soft spinifex, as if you've dipped
into the old knowing welling up from

the sand and desert oaks: the young
flustery stalks, the columns pinned
with needles pointed low; and the grand

masters anchored in the aquifer, each
trunk spread into two or three to frame
the air with brushstrokes like rain.

ii Among the heights

Walking the sandstone rim
of the George Gill Range, humming
'how beautiful are the feet', you stop

as forty or so zebra finches take flight
from under mulga and harlequin mistletoe,
the red and yellow scattered in dry green.

Seven nests in there, each an empty crib
of grass, the lace of lines tethering them
year after year.

And on the plateau of Kings Canyon
with rock fig and blue-clad cycads
between cliffs, near black and parallel

ripples in the slabs by your feet, a sign
from her 'Rock'. Judith Wright sends word
still to *turn a dead sea's leaves and look.*

And in between rust-worn dollops of rock,
the hard heads of old Kata Tjuta, as moisture
drips to the river red gums in the gully

for the woodswallows and firetails
about the valley of the winds, you think
the domes whisper in the shimmer.

iii Around the base of Uluru

Over the plains, over the boulders
and desert bloodwoods, into the red
arkose rock, its gullies and caves, pits

and crevices, into Mutitjulu Waterhole
and Kantju Gorge, into the shaded paths
where the lone butcher-bird sings, where

noisy finches gather and, out by the track,
where masses of cream featherheads sit
all sunlit – the old knowing wells up

from the stories and the spaces
about the centre. Even now it flows,
bearing insight to brim your bones.

Ocean Face, Ocean Mind

After James Drinkwater's *James James Ocean Face* (2018)

What can we truly tell of another's
thoughts, be they flotsam and jetsam

or the wherewithal of wonder filed
in the wilderness of mind? Yours may

be the zest of resonance, a dancing
spectacle, filled with an ocean's quota

of fins, feathers and sediments, for
the yellow band of butterfly fish

and the blue whale's mellow in the depths,
for the light and shadow of a wandering

albatross and the tern on the shore. Now,
may you find yourself in this rock pool,

a mirror like love itself asking over
and over: *tell me your dreams.*

The Art of Doing Things

Nancy Millis AC, MBE, FTSE (1922–2012)

The aroma of the culture from apples in the rolling
green of Somerset, evoked the Victoria Markets
of her childhood, and her father the fruiterer
(*all his ducks were swans*). Like an opening
to another landscape, she knew she belonged.

She chose sick cider to isolate the culprit prokaryote,
to pinprick from pea-green plates to set its doubling
in motion in steel-capped tubes of media. She'd
watch and chart and recall its habits and reactions,
the crude window on the microbe's soul.

The die cast in her early scholarly life to handle
stains and solutions and shaped glass, even the acrid
scent of spent bacteria and molten agar. *I don't
have groundbreaking ideas; I just did the stuff.*
In her sabbatical in Tokyo, she joined two men –

their minds overlapping like a Venn diagram – to
upscale the sphere of Biotechnology. She was positive
as a catalyst for the waste waters in Port Philip Bay
and they'd laud her for that. And more. *Blow that
for a lark* she said and more, for instance,

about the influx of students in '52, *the flood
was nose-high*. To the end, she'd vet ethical checks
on experiments, her company *sharp*. She'd speak
her mind in a man's world – they'd laud her
for that. *The outcomes I want are curious people…*

*If you take on students you should not
    be anything but right at the edge.*

Resolution

After Grace Cossington Smith's *Portrait of Diddy* (c. 1922)

The out-of-sight interplay of light
    and moisture on the pigment white
zinc oxide, made electrons rearrange

in the bonds to form peroxide,
    which scrambled the fibres in the paper
of this portrait of her loving sister.

In the nation's gallery, students hear the story
    of the comings and goings of sub-atomic parts
here in this art; the sketch fully restored.

Electrons in orbitals all around them,
    they think as they leave, like the sparkle

on the surface of the city's lake and trees,
    light striking the cells of all the city's leaves.

Olive with Still Life

After Olive Cotton's *The photographer's shadow* (c. 1935)

We're twinned and twined in love
of purpose. I shade the glare

of your thoughts, see how I fill you
with surprise. Release your heady grip;

tell me again what you hunger for.
You're my boy-next-door, I'm your girl,

we're the best of our past. Right now
I've caught you, an accord in action,

stilled as we are, merged on our speckled
beach in reach of the sea and wrens

about the dunes. As if the light is my dye
to apply or not, the image to outlast us.

The Means to the End

After Elizabeth H. Blackburn, Nobel Prize Laureate, 2009

With the certainty of an arrow, she aimed
to assimilate the new, in each lab from Melbourne
to Cambridge to Yale to Berkeley to UCSF

    Her forefather long loved beetles, as she the word *phenylalanine*

With the warmth of a friend, she sought counsel
from McClintock on maize, Sanger on sequences,
Gall on pond scum, Szostak on yeast cells

    She framed the shapes of organic acids on the walls of her youth

With the stamina of a high-altitude trekker,
and the voracity of a reader, hooked on the hours
and hungry to advance the story of heredity

    She focused on ciliated swirlers and hailed the findings of colleagues

With the insight of an artisan daily accessing
a microscopic world, undaunted by the risks,
alert to the dangers from certain carcinogens

    I could never assume I had done enough, she said

With the methods they gathered, she and her team,
(hot room labelling, culturing and columns, gel
electrophoresis) in lab coat, safety glasses, gloves

    A competent pianist, she designed tests as elegant as a sonata

With notable discussions over conference coffee,
or lunch beyond her lab, a meeting in her office
with a student or a cordial chat in the corridor

    So many experiments, in vitro, in vivo

With probing eyes, she studied the patterns:
the fluorescence in micrographs, the ladder
of stripes in autoradiogram results

    Hers were the means to decode the aglet ends of DNA

Artistry

After Cressida Campbell's *Nasturtiums* (2002)

It's not the array of flowers I'm drawn to
though I've never stopped enjoying their fresh,
bright stance in the garden, as if their cheeks

are full of hellos, as they look you in the face
with their sunny, open, upright disposition.
It's those lines, each curve and straight,

etched and painted as if they hold life:
the rim of each bowl and shadow, the lower
parallel stripes above the succour of water,

the precise tracks defining the cloth. It's
the kind of clarity I'd like to be certain of,
the ability to see past stories I tell myself

as if confusion is the outcome of choice.
It's that cut-through know-how I yearn for,
like the luminous sounds of bellbirds after rain.

The Earth Will Outshine Us

The Lesson

There we were in the photo, heads above the clear
Emmagen Creek, as if we'd been caught in a family
reprieve, any issues dissolved in the ripples. Though

the youngest was already out and up among buttress
roots, focused on his feet and how his teenage hours
set with friends had been reset to the Daintree,

that thick vine draped across the banks like a lifeline
he didn't see. Nor did he think this was where much
happened – we'd think rain on the mountain forms

rock forms soil forms forest over eons. He clambered
on grey limbs, while we felt the bounteous weight
of the place, even with the ferns and palms and lichen

at eye level, that bigger picture of diversity to grasp.
We'd struggled then to frame his young needs. As
I now suspect we failed to point to the fig leaning

in the next photo, its fruits spiralling up the trunk
in hues from leaf green to deep wine. Some design,
this age-old plant with its live-in wasp, and perhaps

we were right to let this story slip and hope he saw
us above the pebbles letting him be, unconditionally,
as the water swirled and held us and nothing more.

The Earth Will Outshine Us

after Elisabeth Cummings's *Arkaroola* (2004)

She's not there now, nor are you, though
some scenes still lodge in your bones.
Wherever you look there's a story edging
the next. Her brush dazzles the text into

lines, into steady and broken passages
and notes of bellow and lore, heavy in
the slanting. You hear echoes of things
said, you see a mirage of heady motion,

as if it's the erosion of earth in time lapse,
the light exposing the rise of dryland teatrees
down by Wywhyana Creek, to the grass trees
up by Sillers Lookout. As if this is a lesson

in seeing all your years vibrate against one
another, the peaks and scatterings, even
the cracks awash in the pleasure of rampant
cadmium. Yet the earth will outshine us all.

And out from the flood plains of Lake Frome
(the white glare of its granules), a falcon
maps the valley and sweeps above the dots
of spinifex, your eyes primed for the swoop.

Beneath the Blue Quandong

Blue as a Brett Whiteley harbour
and a fairy wren's winter brow – by
the path these fruits, some whole
as marbles coated in the sapphire

shade of the Pacific, some peeling
to decay in the dirt. You pause by
the trunk polished grey all the way
to the crown and the whorl of red

ageing in the green, and consider
the cycling of matter, your hands
sifting the years. And what of your
surefired thoughts and beliefs you

vowed then and the small deeds of
recompense or not. And why was it
both of you stepped out of yourselves
here, ready finally to reach for the other.

Links

After James Drinkwater's *Through Tight Bush to the Sea* (2014)

Wind-planed, the plants jostle and jut each other;
each niche leaning into the next, like a family.

It's what you come back to always, so many ways
of seeing them, even the honeyeaters through

the earthy ochres, that stretch in dark salmon,
the burnt remnants, the hierarchy of blue.

Your breath quickens when you reach the edge
of the sea-force on rockface and shore no matter

the time of year. Yet what strikes you now –
not the variations of tone and shape and heath size

as you look around, but the links you can't see:
the volatile molecules and the interplays

under the surface, these untold frequencies
like a score of music to draw from, to draw in.

On William Robinson's Later Harvest

Lavender in the bird bath, scarlet scattered
on the path, the earthy hues of pulled bread
and joined hands, hot orange gum blossom
on a table, sun-kissed peaches on an azure dish.

Hours spent with produce to produce
telltale snippets, the sheen of living looking
simple, looking easy, at one with another,
and always this true clarity.

Brush mark against brush mark to show
each native quality; light glazing each
scene, all yearning spared or solved,
underscoring the two of them, partners

in life, who may be absent but for the feeling
of their presence, the give and take in their
home, having taken the years to hone giving,
in the simply extraordinary business of being.

Four cold white-leghorn eggs in a pan,
a copper cauldron of leafy-green apples,
the faint yellows of rock cakes, and vases
rich with flowers like notes of joyous music.

In Silence

I can protest all I like but soon you won't be
here. Each time I visit there's a sign and today
your V-neck shirt reveals the bones in your chest
pressed close against your thin-stretched skin.
There's too much death and destruction now.

It's disappointing, is all you say of your feeble
muscles; with no strength in your bird-like legs,
none to raise you from your chair. You don't
'rage against the dying of the light'. As we sit,
fires storm through this land. When you listen,

it's with eyes alert for every nuance. When you
speak, it's with words honed well in silence. We
don't talk of the hectares of flames, the ashened
towns, the loss for the living, all the lives lost—
no, we won't. I let your silence envelop us.

Hearing the Grey

The *Karelia Suite* is my undoing but *Valse Triste* is yours, so you both stopped spellbound letting it wash over each of your ninety-plus years. Later you spoke about dying; one to be cremated, burial for the other. No matter who goes first, in the end ashes will be sprinkled on top and under seaside daisies, rampant and chatty. Something to follow step by step; perhaps that's what Sibelius meant in his wistfulness. How your minds have danced together. I remember the afternoon we heard Mahler's *Adagietto* from his 5th, both of you reclining, taking it down into your accomplished bones. Having left your home just now, I'm hearing the grey sea day in the *Ballade* from the top of the hill, the sky full of difficult rain.

From On High

After John Russell's *Toul Rock (Guibel Rock)* (1904–05)

He sets his easel on the grassy sward by yellow
gorse and wandering heath, above mudstone
battered into grey cliffs. On canvas, the broken

headland becomes blue with brilliance,
the aluminate to shine on the sea's mood.

He grinds more pigment with oil, a little resin;
he'll have each pure without loss, each to last
(light-fast, weather-fast) so the sun's rays

are always just so. There's Toul Rock with
its window on the water, shimmering.

Two decades he's known the bustle and calm
of bays and inlets, red sails and fishermen;
himself a sailor, a boatbuilder. He brushes

for an impression as rich as the real: the house
and garden for Marianna his love, their five sons

and Jeanne. Each touch, each edge and spread
this way and that, he'll square with his flat dab
and stroke into every nook: their simple lives

on Belle-Île. Not Paris, nor Sydney, it's here
he can paint their everyday. Yesterday's ride

with Marianna, the children at play, the flowers
at Goulphar, the boats. He's here at the height
of his artistry en plein air. Like our best days

of giving, he'll frame this and set us in
the high-key flow of an unfading summer.

In Tumult

In memory of Denise Frost, 1947–2015
After Philip Wolfhagen's *Surface Tension #3*

His canvas beside her. *How the textures leap
close*, she said. I think of a water strider's long
legs spread out above the surface, but this

is no pond's tension, nor is it the force and fury
of white water, drowning cries. They wrap around
you, his waxed blues, and lock like the darkest

hours of racing thought, the lurch and roll and curl.
When we spoke, even her eyes listened then. I see
them still and wonder have I loved enough.

He loved to brush rhythms (the drama of *Gloriana*)
on linen, his strip of sea without bird or boat and
fading to the palest sky. She knew art, I knew

briefly the light she cast. But the sudden
shocking loss of her, so young still, churned
like an ocean in tumult, the tears in his sea. Yet,

after the cathedral of grief, spoken and sung,
this then, her parting gift: that we would leave
with the strain and swirl of 'Here Comes the Sun'.

Green Tea

I hold it daily, this cup you gave
me. We'd been to the gallery, met

the potter, her wares, the glazes.
The cup's aqua and ochre tones

are like earth and sea on a quiet
day. The well of green tea it holds

brightens like a swell of kindness.
I've not tired of the cup's shape,

its wide mouth, generous handle
and height, the swirls and overlap

of colours on the outer and inner
surfaces.   And most of all, how

it brings back that day and since,
when I've held you close.

Skin to Skin

Blaze and Stone

On Messiaen's *Quartet for the End of Time* (1940)

Into the prison camp in Silesia, Messiaen
brought an angel cloaked in cloud, scored
rainbows into crystals, transposed harmony
into cascades of orange-blue calm. Mixed
though with dissonance, the most ungodly
vibrations to the ear, as if that angel had
run amok. From the cold and hunger, Olivier's
hair and teeth fell out, no wonder. Not though

his faith. With swollen fingers, he played
the dance of fury, a messiah with his chosen
three. They heard how he'd written in love,
saw how it gave them wings. All because
he'd listened to birdsong for hours
and wrote down every feathered note.

Swifts in the Sclerophyll

You may marvel at the feathers:
those streaks of red above and below
the beak, the cheek and crown washed
in blue, some lemon splashed about,
the remarkable greens, the long fit
of a scarlet-trimmed tail. You may

consider the ruffle of stamens, the rub
of nectar in *robusta, maculata, gummifera*
and other woodland trees, the grey box
and white, the blackbutt and ironbark.
Our evergreens. You may suppose when
it first began, this blossoming of purpose:

the birds from across Bass Strait to lean
into flower after flower and lerp, over
winter. The sure, swift flights. You might
stop simply to be under their busyness
to know the price of these feasts,
and how and why they must persist.

Facing the Music

No sign of possums unsettled in the treescape
this wintry grey day, though there's lantana about,
that clever feral, ever in flower. A kookaburra sits,

a study in focus, his breast puffed Buddha-like
on a branch of a bloodwood. The track takes
me down to smooth trunks rising at eye level

from the old, solid bedrock and brings me to face
finally, an acceptance of ageing I was at pains
to evade. Lorikeets are feasting in spotted gums,

high like the notes of the prelude in Beethoven's
solemn mass, before the violin's descent to, and in
the blessing, that air-light waltz above the clouds

bringing those ethereal, *lebensfreude* feelings
he gifted the world in this, his later-period piece.
Now near Whitebridge, young fiddleheads reach up

in a stream of light from the great weight of their
fronds, as a whipbird flits across my path to vanish
past a quiver of grass with a quick whirr.

In Our Name

No gunshot wound or knife, no broken
jaw or neck from a shameful attack or car
crash: you've slipped under the barriers

so far, under the block of cancer, or any
autoimmune or lifestyle disease. Well
done you, in working order still; eyes,

ears doing their best with a slow loss, legs
looking to stride, arms at ease, stomach
with habitual grumbles, those lower lips

humming, heart on track to keep pace,
lungs reminding me to remember the gift
of this ordinary moment. You've caused

me scant trouble, nothing I haven't made
by actions, with fear the star of alignment.
A handful of hospital times, forgotten

now except the underlying gratitude.
Look how we've lived, salt of the earth,
some small offering to the world. So, are

you content then with whatever I've
managed to achieve or done in our name,
given these years, all three-score-and-ten?

Beef Tea Heirloom

A Schauer *Australian Cookery Book*
fifteenth impression: cover torn, binding
tattered, pages misaligned, some creased,
some ripped from her hurried use.

Between the recipes for small cakes,
a blank cheque and in faint purple pencil,
her winning version of rock cakes with
extra lemon zest and sugar crust.

In the savoury section, three small black
&whites: my brother, aged eight in cricket
gear, then at his wedding, and my sister
just at the door of our leaning outhouse.

According to the insert at page 558, my
mother was joint winner in the state's
bronze foursomes championship in golf.
She'd serve rich trifles in her prize crystal.

Legally blind in her final year, she asked for
beef tea. I note now from the Invalid Cookery
pages, a beaten egg yolk and white added
separately at boiling point fortifies the broth.

Inside the back cover, a yellowed cutting:
how to join the Women's Royal Australian
Army Corps and on the reverse: *Tested
recipes you will find very easy to follow.*

St Lucia, 1969

That day I took home a huge
bunch of Cootamundra wattle
from the university grounds
and gave it to my mother –
I'd never seen such profusion,
nor she. I can still see her face.
It was as if the sun had come,
the baking and sewing done,
the washing in, and all she
had to do then, was sing.

Her Hands

Imaged on the screen, skin with pigment
and wan patches. Skin too thin, too loose
and puckered in folds across the joints
and over the veins, like a flesh-toned

X-ray. Hands she set to bake and sew,
to shop and scrub and fix, to drive and
mend and plant, to pat and soothe, to
turn the pages of a book, to write

to me. Hands I held through her final
breath, imaged on the screen for all
of us here, and now down in my lap
I see my mother's hands are mine.

Greengrocer

When I told him my mother had passed
and he'd no longer need to cut pumpkin
into pieces she could manage, I could tell
by his eyes how sad he was at the news,
though it could've reminded him of someone
else, someone sick or close to being lost to him.

She liked her vegies; she could chop potato,
carrot, could shell peas. I told him how much
she valued his help and his eyes took on a new
hue as his face shone. He'd only ever charged
her for the pieces she'd eat, not the rest he'd
compost, he was that kind of village grocer.

Skin to Skin

A new head nestled
by your neck, the love
of your daughter's labour
to cup with your hand;
her hair a light sheen, her
slow milky sighs, her body
huddled into your chest.

And mid-century say,
may corals bloom and rains
lull, and the winds soothe
her face; and may she lie
skin to skin with her other
on the earth we've willed
to hold and brim with life.

Toddler with Neptune's Necklace

She bends to waft her fingers in the rock pool,
lingers there, as if she's listening
to a lullaby before sleep. I break off

a strand, her eyes follow its thin float.
She picks it up, squeezes a bead
then another, thumb and first finger

on the firm baubles. She turns them,
till she spots how light is caught like honey
beyond the dark marks of the skin.

I point to limpets stuck like cone hats
and the zebra snail at the end of its track,
sand piled on the sides of its narrow winding

path. She eyes other crop on the rock
and now, when I hoist her up onto the ledge,
she discovers how to glide over

the lumpy cover of necklaces and slip
down into the water; the chill rising to her chest.
I point to the fleeting shadows of small fish

but she wants the ledge, to toe-grip the algae
before she drops; we do this again and again,
and each time her shrieks spell a new thrill.

Now She's Three

She draws her first M, dribbles its legs
down the page, states what it stands for
and whom, her eyes beady as a bird's.

Your skin's falling off your face, she says.
What will be there when it goes? I ask.
She drops her head, lowers her voice.
Blood Nan. Blood.
                        When I pretend
to be the one who won't go to day care,
she strokes my hair, whispers who I'd play
with, where I'd sit at lunch, how I'd sink
my spoon into potato mash and after,
go outside on a bear hunt.
                        *I can't make tears
like that*, I say through her howling. *Can
I have some of yours? Look*, as I slap
my cheek. *See, no tears*. I belt my other
cheek, laughter launches from her depths:
do it again Nanny, do it again.
                        She looks askance
at my sketch of a dark bewitcher. *But for
your drawing my love*, she throws a belly-load
of laughs to the ceiling, clutching your page
hard to her chest.
                        She brushes
the butcher's paper in fields of orange,
hot pink and blue, like Hockney's *Imagining
the Grand Canyon*, lit small and waiting for trees.

                          Listening to you
on piano, she closes her eyes. Her feet twirl,
her hands curl and reach, her body turns
in tune with the notes as if she's learnt already
where to lose and where to find herself.

Now She's Four

She makes a beeline for non-fiction
in the library after the shock of the black
snake sunning by Glenrock Lagoon.

She's pulled by magnets and kaleidoscopes,
tests them in the garden, and spots
dragonflies and the moon. She holds

a tape measure over any surface, peering
at the numbers. She designs shapes,
sticks paper to clothe tiny figures

without looking up. She slopes a column
of cardboard from a chair to the floor, adds
more around the room for a marble run.

She mixes ingredients into potions, pours dyed
water into cups (without a spill) and watches.
She likes the sound of *porcelain*.

I read the book on bees to her though
she doesn't eat honey and chooses flowers
lit with the warmer end of the spectrum.

Track Drift

Waiting

The candle is lit. He's facing the camera;
we see his dark-rimmed, square-framed
glasses, his bounteous, black hair.
He might've just asked her to marry
him, so keen in his three-piece suit.

She's focusing on his curled right hand,
its silken skin, his fingers long enough
for any octave. She might be speaking,
her mouth caught half open, although
more likely it's a moment of laughter.

They each have a glass half-filled for some
celebration, but there's no cutlery on the table
before the rattan screen of the restaurant.
She wears a green waist-length jacket over
a red dress with a blaze of blue, '70s style.

You can feel the excitement, in the way
they're fresh for each other and the way
she leans into him, her hair all blonde and
long and down past the covered button
of her jacket, with its only one fastener.

Walking

i

If you'd come early in the winter wood,
you'd have noticed how red and supple
were the pine needles, and how slow
the wake of a pelican by the water's edge.

You'd have heard firetails in leaf litter,
gang-gangs at berries, a few walkers
near the first flowering wattles, and seen
grey gathered above the western range.

ii

Towards the heavens inflamed
with rays of light, the astronomical
lines of eight minutes from the sun.

In eight minutes, I cross the wooden
bridge crusted with frost, the call
of a yellow robin filling the cold air.

Reunion

There's the school anthem in Latin with
all the pomp of a Verdi march – the notes

and melody line come easily though
I haven't heard it for decades nor been

back in the airy space of this chapel. Faces
I wouldn't recognise walk towards me,

each with the same gait, same voice,
same tilt of the head as I saw back then.

None of us seems to care what we do
or have done, we're not looking past

each other as we once did, nor judging,
finally. It's about being here and giving,

and grappling again with this Latin
I know no more about now, than then.

Trees

In memory of Helen Dowling (1926–2018)

i

The steps to her backyard of mallee trees—
three worn blocks of sandstone from the river
valley of their earlier home; I remember them

now, slabs of grey, smooth and soft underfoot.
From the kitchen window, we'd watch pardalotes
in their clay nest. And how she took small steps

before me on the track, frailer and more bent,
how she spoke of not remembering. But stopped
at a gum, threw out her arms with joy for the age

of it, as she did that rocky outcrop she bent to.
I like a tree that isn't hemmed in, she said. And
I thought we were at Tidbinbilla to hear lyrebirds.

ii

She'd shown me snow gums, how they twist
high on ranges cradling frost plains. And how
the wind pillowed snow, lulled birds, cajoled

itself overnight above the young river.
We walked by heath in pallets of cream
to green, by swaths of yellow leaf or herb,

pink grasses and patches in indigo to brown
down to the wetland's black earth. She knew
the mountain huts and the trackless climb

to granite monoliths over sweeping scenes;
how to read the High Country, its valleys
and habits; even how the trees speak.

iii

Her room has a small balcony, the azalea
in the blue and white china pot she took
from her home, now just hanging on.

Oh, I'm content here, she says. *Look I have
trees.* She waves at the tall eucalypts beyond.
I think that I shall never see a poem lovely

as a tree, she quotes. I tell her again we've
moved to near the ocean. *After we'd learnt
to swim, Dad had us holiday in the mountains.*

And then come more memories: birding
with her sister, years of farming (the nights
so black by the Goodradigbee River), the fresh

scent of ribbon gums. Soon she won't know
me. But today she smiled when I left, her face
serene as if she was *out with the big gums*.

Beech (*Fagus sylvatica*)

for Maggie

You're seated on a fallen log in a beech wood
of your choosing, having chosen this life, this

place, far from your birthplace, that's taken
me a lifetime to visit. Having travelled an earth

-full of triumph and trial, your feet settled just
now among the ivy and spent brown, below

the mosaic of leaves, layered and lustrous. And
each time we've met over the years is an oasis

of calm and concern and conviction I hold close.
True to nature, you're steadfast as the beech.

By the Hawkesbury

Halfway stop midweek in Brooklyn,
we walk the avenue of courtly palms
to the counter of choice seafood.

We choose flathead from this river,
take it to a bench by Lookout Bay,
the flesh light and luscious.

Our words float like the years about
the flow and the islands and the lavish
foliage, by this butter-smooth sandstone.

It's like being immersed in salad days,
and suddenly this rises to the surface:
the zest, surprise and sureness of you.

Track Drift

Swaths of colour-clad cyclists whirr past, six
at a time more or less and a motley of walkers

in early light on the Fernleigh Track. Dear B,
we took the full span of the path one midday,

our talk going where it willed. Birds too are absent
now, silenced by waves of heady cicada vibrato.

And little said of our Canberra years: absorbed in
precise procedures (solutions, the centrifuge room,

the assays); the bamboo potted on our director's
desk, his long career neatly before him, while ours

bent to the clutter and charting of children. On
the periphery of each other's lives then, yet

back into synchrony by the old train line here,
clear as the veneer of ochre waxing the angophoras.

We stepped beneath the busy spring canopy in tune
with the years' course, what we left and carry still.

Foresight

There's one man slumped like a C
in the front seat; another leans against
a pole, his face dark on the yellow
of his jacket. Others in hi-vis, sombre
as the fog outside, tumble into the city.

They enter: the nurse with her child,
the woman plus Sudoku, the girls in gym
wear, the academic in suit and gloves,
all of us collected in this moment. I'm
en route to the office, my final career

counting the mothering days that sit
needle-firm in my compass. I centre
on the drive of today's rosella: like
a flare from the dewy grass with his
winter-bright breast, his eyes poised.

Chaos on a Canvas

after John Wolseley's *Distant glimpses of the great floodplain seen through a veil of trees and hanging vines* (2017)

This isn't Blue Mud Bay; tracks are overgrown
    and the second yield of seeds blown away
like the first, for the scurry and silence of ants
    and beetles. A rush of wings and a butcher-bird
lands with a cicada in its beak. Fan-flower
    and glycine pea shower their lilac near a ground
-breaking spectacle of asparagus fern, that lowly
    queen of the weeds. Vines trail, lashing themselves
onto anything; and you're reminded of how
    much you don't know, like the shades of green.

You pass a wall of white flowers three metres
    high and think of the curves in tubers,
rhizomes and roots; blue skies occupy you
    though your socks are wicks in wet shoes
and mosquitoes settle on your skin. A myriad
    of fingerling seedlings, their straggly shoots
leaning in watery bounty, all part of the matrix
    given by the gods. We're like that you guess,
good enough always, shining sometimes like
    the Klein blue of dianella or the golden ball

of wombat berry. Pole-straight trunks stand
   in unpuckered ochre, their old *propinqua* bark
strewn under the cicadas' clamour. This is another
   harvest, another hallelujah. There's a hillside
filled with hands of maiden hair, blessings
   tethered in air and swaying in the breeze. Chaos
on a canvas will last longer than the disorder
   in the bush from this La Niña season. And now,
small pale butterflies dart among the flatweeds
   as if in time to Ross Edwards' *Ecstatic Dances*.

Notes

For the poem 'The Matter of Covid-19': Australia's borders closed on 20 March 2020 in response to the Covid-19 pandemic.

In 'Under the Microscope', italicised lines are from the Papers of Isobel Bennett, National Library of Australia MS 9348.

In '*The Art of Doing Things*', italicised words are from those spoken by Nancy Millis in https://nla.gov.au/nla.obj-219635303/listen Millis, Nancy F & Linn, Rob. (2010). Nancy Millis interviewed by Rob Linn.

The title of 'The Means to the End' is taken from Nobel Lecture 2009 by Elizabeth H. Blackburn, *Telomeres and Telomerase: The Means to the End*. The poem's content was adapted from Elizabeth Blackburn's Nobel Lecture 2009 and the book *Elizabeth Blackburn and the Story of Telomeres: Deciphering the Ends of DNA* by Catherine Brady, MIT Press, Cambridge, Massachusetts, USA, 2007.

The words quoted in 'In Silence' are taken from Dylan Thomas's poem 'Do Not Go Gentle Into That Good Night'.

Acknowledgements

I am indebted to Jean Kent for her invaluable feedback, and her generous, ongoing support. And to Brook Emery for his interest, guidance and endorsement. Also, I'd like to thank the members of the Hunter Writers Centre Poetry Group, the Focus poets and Poetry at the Pub, Newcastle, for their comments and camaraderie. I found the following workshops particularly valuable: Poetry & Nature: Poetic responses to the work of Ash Island's Scott Sisters with Judy Johnson, Online Feedback: Poetry with Judith Beveridge, and Online: Writing Poetry with Vanessa Kirkpatrick. And I'd like to thank Ruth Cotton and Brenda Proudfoot for their continuing friendship and encouragement.

I am grateful to the editors of the anthologies and journals in which the following poems appeared:

'Beef Tea Heirloom' in *Not Very Quiet* Issue 3, September 2018

'Swifts in the Sclerophyll' in *Australian Poetry Collaboration* #29, 2018

'With the Moths on Ash Island' in *Shuffle*, 2019 and nominated for Best Writing Award in the Microflix Awards, 2020

'Underground' in *Not Very Quiet* Issue 5, September 2019

'In Tumult' in *Grieve* Volume 7, 2019

'From On High' in *Antipodes* Volume 33, Number 2, 2019

'The Earth Will Outshine Us' in *Westerly* Volume 64, Number 1, 2019 and subsequently in *Australian Poetry Anthology* Volume 8, 2020

'Under the Brisbane Quandong' in *Westerly* Volume 64, Number 2, 2019

'KI Postscript' in #authorsforfireys, *Westerly* online, 2020

'Going Home' in *Not Very Quiet* Issue 6, March 2020

'In Silence' in *I Protest! Poems of Dissent*, Ginninderra Press, 2020

'The Lesson' in *Not Very Quiet* Issue 7, September 2020

'On William Robinson's Later Harvest' in 2020 ACU Prize for Poetry Chapbook

'Circuit, Blackheath' in *Messages from the Embers*, 2020

'The Art of Doing Things' in *Blue Nib*, 2020

'Under the Microscope' in *Science Write Now*, 2020

'Toddler with Neptune's Necklace' in *This Gift, This Poem*, Puncher & Wattmann, 2021

'About the Centre, Even Now' won the Alice Sinclair Prize for Poetry 2020.

www.ingramcontent.com/pod-product-compliance
Lightning Source LLC
Chambersburg PA
CBHW062147100526
44589CB00014B/1716

www.ingramcontent.com/pod-product-compliance
Lightning Source LLC
Chambersburg PA
CBHW062150100526
44589CB00014B/1766